DAVID

THE FEARLESS FIGHTER

TOLD BY CARINE MACKENZIE
ILLUSTRATIONS BY FRED APPS

Copyright © 1996 Carine Mackenzie
ISBN: 978-1-85792-198-4
Reprinted 2001, 2004, 2007, 2009, 2012
Published by Christian Focus Publications, Geanies House,
Fearn, Tain, Ross-shire, IV20 1TW, Scotland, U.K.
www.christianfocus.com
Printed in China

David was the youngest son in a large family of eight boys. Their father Jesse owned lots of sheep and David's job was to look after these sheep – leading them to find pasture to graze, water to drink and protecting them from danger.

Some of David's older brothers were soldiers in the army of King Saul – they were big and strong and brave.

David was brave too. His sheep grazed out in the wilderness where wild animals lurked. Once a lion came and stole a lamb from the flock. David chased the lion, caught it by its long hair and rescued the lamb from its mouth. He then killed the lion to protect his sheep. Another time a big bear came to try to take a young lamb. David fearlessly went after the bear and rescued the lamb. David looked after his sheep very well.

One day David was called home while he was working in the fields with the sheep. His father had an important visitor – Samuel the priest. Samuel had been told by God to go to Jesse's house. One of Jesse's sons was God's choice for the next king.

One by one Jesse's other sons were introduced to Samuel. They were fine and handsome but they were not God's choice. Samuel had to turn each of them down. 'Have you no other sons?' he asked.

'Yes,' replied Jesse. 'There is David, the youngest. He is out looking after the sheep.'

Fetch him,' said Samuel. 'We will not sit down until he comes.'

David came in from the field, glowing with good health. He was very handsome. God told Samuel, 'This is the one. Anoint him as king.'

So Samuel took a container of oil and poured some on David's head, to show that he had been chosen by God to be the king in the future.

All his brothers were present and watched as Samuel anointed David. From that day, the Spirit of God was with David in a powerful way.

David was a talented musician. He could play the harp and sing. He had composed many songs or psalms which expressed his love for God.

'The Lord is my shepherd; I shall not want,' sang David. 'He makes me to lie down in green pastures, he leads me beside still waters.' David, as a shepherd, could understand the loving care that God gave to him.

King Saul was in a bad temper. Evil thoughts troubled his mind. 'We should find a skilful harp player to come and play for Saul. That would soothe his mind and cheer him up,' thought Saul's advisers.

Someone suggested, 'One of Jesse's sons is a really good harp player – a brave and wise young man too.'

So David was summoned by the king. Jesse sent David off with a donkey laden with gifts – bread, wine and meat. David's harp playing refreshed Saul and drove away the evil thoughts.

Saul and his army were at war with the Philistines who wanted to take over the land. The Philistine army had one soldier who was mightier than all the others. He was called Goliath. He was a huge giant – over three metres tall.

Goliath came from his camp – over the valley – and shouted across to the soldiers of Saul's army, 'Choose a man to come and fight me. If I beat your man then you will be our servants.'

Saul and his soldiers, including David's three older brothers, were all scared.

Father Jesse was concerned about his three sons at the battle front with King Saul. One day he called young David in. 'Go and see your brothers,' Jesse told David. 'Take these ten cheeses to their group captain and see how they are getting on.'

David set off early next morning to the battle field, and made his way among the ranks of soldiers to find his three brothers.

As he was talking to them, Goliath the giant came out of the camp to shout abuse across the valley to King Saul's army. All King Saul's soldiers ran back afraid; no one wanted to take up the challenge to fight huge Goliath.

'If someone managed to beat Goliath, what would be his reward?' David asked some of the men around. 'The King will make him very rich; he will give him one of his daughters for a wife; his family won't have to pay taxes,' was the reply.

David was very interested. His brothers were annoyed. 'Who do you think you are? You should be back home looking after your sheep. You just came here to see some of the action.'

'What harm have I done?' replied David. He would not leave the matter alone and asked other men – he got the same answer.

King Saul heard David was in the camp and that he was asking questions. David was summoned to the King's tent.

'Don't let your army lose heart because of this giant Goliath. I will go and fight him,' declared David.

'You can not fight against such an experienced soldier,' objected Saul. 'You are just a boy.'

David told him how he had killed a lion and a bear all alone when he was looking after his father's sheep. 'The same God who saved me from being killed by the lion and the bear, will keep me safe when I fight Goliath, the Philistine,' said David confidently.

'Go ahead,' ordered Saul. 'The Lord be with you.'

David was dressed just as a simple shepherd.

'Put on my uniform,' said Saul, 'You will need armour. Use mine.'

He dressed David in his heavy coat of armour and gave him his bronze helmet.

David fastened his sword at his side and then tried to walk around. He could hardly move. They were so heavy and awkward that David felt very clumsy.

'I cannot use these,' he told Saul. 'I am just not used to them.' So he took off all the armour and the helmet and went to fight Goliath in his shepherd's clothes.

In one hand was the staff that he used as a shepherd to pull a sheep from a craggy crevice or catch a lamb when it was straying.

He went down to the stream and picked out five smooth stones and put them in the pouch of his shepherd's bag.

His weapon was the sling that he used to fire stones – to frighten off wild animals that would be snooping round the flock.

When Goliath saw the young shepherd boy coming towards him with a small sling, he was absolutely livid. He shouted taunts at David. David replied bravely, 'You come to fight with a sword and a spear and a javelin. But I come to fight in the name of the Lord God. He will help me to win. The battle is the Lord's. He will give all of you into our hands.'

The Philistine army advanced, but quick as lightening David darted forward. He reached into his bag for one of the stones, slung a shot and struck Goliath in the middle of the forehead.

The stone sank right down into his head and he fell down on his face – dead.

Young David with a sling and one stone had completely defeated the massive Philistine soldier with all his armour and weapons.

David ran up to Goliath's body, pulled his sword from its scabbard and used it to cut off Goliath's head.

The Philistine soldiers were in complete shock. Their champion had been killed by a young shepherd boy. What would happen to them now? They turned and ran for their lives.

Saul's army were in hot pursuit – chasing them all the way back to the cities of Gath and Ekron. They claimed all the things the Philistines had left behind in their camp – David took possession of Goliath's weapons as his spoil of war.

David was a hero. From then on he became a soldier instead of a shepherd. He was such a successful soldier that Saul soon promoted him to a high rank. When the army returned to the city of Jerusalem after the war, the women lined the streets cheering King Saul and the army. News of David's triumph had reached the city. The women were singing and dancing.

The song they sung went like this:

> *'Saul has slain his thousands*
> *and David his tens of thousands.'*

This made Saul jealous and angry. 'They are giving David more credit than me,' he muttered. He was so jealous that he tried to kill David, but God kept David safe.

God was in control of David's life. He kept him safe when he was working as a shepherd. David knew that the Lord was a good shepherd to him.

God still looks after his children like a shepherd. 'I am the good shepherd,' said Jesus. God used weak, young David to fight the evil Goliath. He still uses weak things and people for his purpose. With God on our side we will be able to fight against Satan, the evil one. We have been given a sword to do this – the sword of the Spirit which is the Word of God.

David put his trust in God. We should do the same.